# PRISONERS
# OF OUR OWN
# BELIEFS

# PRISONERS
# OF OUR OWN
# BELIEFS

**Sometimes I Fear I Have Created A
Prison, And The Walls Are My Inability
To Believe In Myself.**

# Gary Parent

Library of Congress Cataloging-in-Publication Data

Parent, Gary

Prisoners of Our Own Beliefs : Awaken to a New Freedom of Endless Potential, Passion & Power

1. Self- Help 2. Psychology

First Printing

ISBN 0-9709321-5-4

Network 3000 Publishing, 3432 Denmark Ave. #108, Eagan, Minnesota 55123 USA

Printed in the United States of America

# *<u>Acknowledgements</u> *

Cover Design - Gary Parent

Photographs - TERELAR - Teresa & Larry Ayotte

Editor - Paul J. Shanley

# What You Hide From, You Become A Prisoner To

**Dedicated To Those**

**Who**

**Stand Up And Scream,**

**"Onward!  Onward!"**

**Step By Step.**

# CONTENTS

# CONTENTS

# CONTENTS

WE ALL HAVE DEFINING MOMENTS
IN OUR LIVES. EACH ONE PUTS
US ON A NEW PATH, ~~FIRST IS~~
~~US ON~~ A NEW JOURNEY,
IT COULD BE A LOSS OF A JOB
THE ~~ENDOR~~ ENDING OF A RELATIONSHIP
PYSHICAL OR MENTAL ABUSE,
THE LOSS OF A LOVED ONE OR A
NEAR DEATH EXPERIENCE.
IT CAN BE ANYTHING THAT CHANGES
NOT ONLY HOW YOU SEE THE WORLD
BUT HOW YOU FIT IN IT.
THIS PATH, THIS JOURNEY WILL DO
ONE OF TWO THINGS. IT WILL CRUSH
YOU OR IT WILL MAKE YOU STRONGER.
ALL OF MINE CRUSHED ME UNTIL
I WAS IN AN AUTOMOBILE ACCIDENT
IN 1979, IT WAS THEN, AND IS TODAY
THE SINGLE MOST DEVASTATING AND
IMPORTANT EVENT IN MY LIFE
IT CREATED A TRIGGER POINT IN
ME THAT NOT ONLY DEFINES WHO
I AM, IT ALOUD ME TO STAND UP
INSIDE MYSELF AND FACE MY GREATEST
~~FEAR~~ "MY BELIEF IN MYSELF" IT MADE
ME ~~REALIZE~~ THAT NO MATTER WHAT
OR WHO I AM, PEOPLE WILL STILL

GATHER AROUND ME AND THE
TRUER I AM TO MYSELF AND
WHAT I WANT IN LIFE. THE GREATER
MY EXPERIENCES IN LIFE HAVE BECOME. ✻
   THERE IS A CERTAIN CALMNESS
THAT HAS COME OVER ME, THAT HELPED
ME UNDERSTAND THAT IT IS OKAY TO BE ME,

THERE WERE TWO THINGS I ALWAYS
WANTED TO BE IN LIFE
   AN ARTIST AND A WRITER
   MY CIRCLE OF INFLUENCE CONVINCED
ME THAT THEIR WAS NO MONEY IN BEING
AN ARTIST
      "THERE IS"
I HAVE BEEN A PROFESSIONAL ARTIST SINCE 1986
   AND SCHOOL TAUGHT ME THAT WHEN YOU
ARE A FAILING STUDENT BEING A WRITER
IS IMPOSIBLE  "IT IS'NT
   I FOUND OUT AT AGE 38 THAT I AM
DYSLEXIC SO WITH THE REALIZATION
OF THAT I READ MY FIRST BOOK
AT AGE 46 THEN AT AGE 50 I BEGAN
WRITING PRISONERS OF OUR OWN
BELIEFS.
   NEVER LET ANYONE'S OPIONION OF
YOU DETERMAND WHO YOU ARE OR WHAT

16

YOU WILL DO IN YOUR LIFE

IT IS IMPOSSIBLE TO FAIL IF YOU
NEVER QUIT.

NO REGRET, NO RETREAT, NO SURRENDER

I Wish To Thank All
The
Dream Stealers
And
Dream Builders
In My Life.
Without The
Challenges Of The
One,
And The Belief In
Me Of
The Other, I Would
Not Be Who I Am
Today,
And
This Book Would
Not Exist.

# Listen To Your Inner Voice.

# It Is Your Only True Guide.

# Introduction

## Meeting The Most Important

## Person In Your Life.

One day, I was introduced to some people who changed my life forever. They did what no one else had ever done. They believed in me long enough for me to believe in myself.

That's what true friends do.

They introduced me to the single most important person I had ever met in my life. He took me to seminars to hear incredible people speak about life, love, passion, hope, the future, and a dream. He took me to book stores to learn new things, new ideas, new thoughts, and buy books, tapes, and CDs, which I had never done before. In fact, I had never read a book, ever, until I was 46 years old, and that took a year and a half of coaxing. Since then, I have never looked back. Now I read at least fifteen minutes a day. My day is never complete unless I read so I can learn something new every day.

If you are wondering who the single most important person in my life was, I would love to tell you. I only hope that, someday, you meet the person who changes your life. As it did mine.

That person was me.

And my life has not been, and will not ever be, the same ever again. In fact, even though my handprinted letter at the start of this book is full of mistakes, three years ago I could not have written it.

Life is a decision. When will you make a decision to change your life?

The Reward Of The Goal

Is Only Exceeded By

The Memory Of The

Journey.

# Eleven Steps To

# Your Emotional Freedom

# It All Begins

# With Awareness

# 1

# Awareness

## Just Whose Life Is This, Anyway?

The first challenge you will face is a test of discovery. Discovering who you are and that you have worth. That you are worthwhile--and you are!

The second challenge you will face is a test of courage, strength, and faith within yourself. This is the greatest challenge you will ever face. Why? Because you have a lack of awareness not only of who you are, but what you want to do with your life. And it's no wonder. Every time you turn around, someone is saying something about you, and not just to someone else, but to your face. You become so used to it, you not only accept it, you actually expect it.

The key to changing this is listening, truly listening, to what's being said to you and about you.

Is it positive, or is it negative? Does it make you feel good or bad? Does it make you feel you're moving in a forward direction? That you can achieve anything?

Or does it destroy your ambition, leaving you flat, with no energy, making it seem impossible to achieve your goals?

If I were to ask you one question, it would be this-- which one are you? Do you criticize, condemn, and complain about everyone around you, including yourself?

Or do you praise and promote everyone around you, including yourself?

To discover which one you are, just remember--people will always reflect back to you what you project to them. Like a mirror which reflects your face back to you, life reflects your emotions back to you.

So what do you say to yourself? What does that little voice in your head tell you when you look in the mirror, or when you get mad at yourself? Do you criticize, condemn, and complain about everyone around you, including yourself? Or do you praise and promote everyone around you, including yourself? I'll bet if your friends said the things to you that you say to yourself, they wouldn't be your friends for very long.

So be kind to yourself. You're definitely worth it.

Always praise and promote yourself and others. Just like when people ask, "Where should I invest my time and my money?" There is only one answer to a question like that—

IN YOURSELF.

IN YOURSELF.

Just live life on your own terms. Many people are not living their lives at all. They're just going through the motions,
day after day.

So dare to be different. Read books. Listen to CDs or educational tapes. Attend seminars. Learn new things that excite you, no matter what other people say or think.

Live life. Go for it. Grab life before life grabs you. Just whose life is it, anyway? Stop listening to those who criticize, condemn, and complain, not only about you, but to you. And always remember--

YOU ARE ONE OF A KIND!

You will always get from life what you believe you deserve. Whether your beliefs are good, bad, or indifferent, your life will always gravitate in the directions that you see yourself in the world. Did you ever wonder where your beliefs came from in the first place? They came from your Circle of Influence.

One of the keys to being happy in life is to stop letting your Circle of Influence tell you what you can and can not do, or be, or have, in or with your life. Don't let them set your limits. You know what you can do, and what you truly want to do, in and with your life, better than they ever will. It's time to stand up inside yourself and set your dreams on fire!

Live, love, and laugh often because life is short, and you're too awesome to let your Circle of Influence control your emotions and push you away from your goals.

Part 2 is about knowing and understanding who your Circle of Influence is, and how they have, and still do, put limits on your life. Even as you are reading this book. So read on, and learn well, because your future depends on it.

## Circle of Influence

# Your Beliefs Are The Backbone Of Your Success

# 2

# Circle of Influence

## The Power of Those Around You

Life is a journey. Your experiences make your life, your journey, uniquely yours.

A famous scientist, Sir Isaac Newton, said that every action has an equal and opposite reaction. He spoke of the physical world. But the social world works the same way. You have self-doubt because you fear the social reaction your decisions will cause in your Circle of Influence. Your fear holds you prisoner.

You live in, and with, fear, so you avoid making decisions. This avoidance is dangerous to your physical, mental, and spiritual health. This avoidance may cause you to take a lifetime to awaken from what will seem like a long sleep or a dream. A life-altering experience may change your outlook. You may drift through years of your life and wake up saying, "This is not how I wanted my life to be. This is not what I wanted to do with my life. How did I get where I am?"

But what is an experience? What does it do for you? What makes you remember an experience?

An experience is an emotional response to something, or someone that happened to you, a memory. Sight, sound, touch, taste, or smell trigger your emotional response to that memory. Your five senses, and your

Circle of Influence, are how you learn everything you know, and everything you ever will know.

The more intense your emotional response is to a memorable experience, the longer and more intense your reaction will be to that memory.

Your emotional experiences guide you through life. You use those experiences to determine what, and whom you like and dislike. Those experiences form all of your beliefs and disbeliefs. You use those experiences every minute of every day. These experiences determine the life you have led up to now, and the life you will lead in all of your tomorrows.

So if you are trying to make decisions in your life, and your emotions are out of your control, then your decisions are out of your control.

The more out-of-control your emotions and decisions are, the greater is the risk that you will make a mistake about the direction you want your life and your future to go in.

Your emotions are an invisible field of protection that surrounds you. The words and body language your Circle of Influence uses around you every day trigger your invisible field of protection in a positive way or a negative way.

The more you agree with your Circle of Influence, the more enjoyment you get when you expand into their conversation, actions, or space.

But if your Circle of Influence says or does something offensive or frightening, you may find you will withdraw, or even run, from your Circle of Influence.

What happens is this--it becomes impossible to store all your experiences in your conscious mind. So you store them in your subconscious mind. This is simple to prove. All you need to do is be hypnotized, and your subconscious memories will spring to life as if they happened yesterday. So your experiences are still there, and you still use them every day to make the decisions that shape your present life and future.

Storing and using subconscious experiences can be dangerous, because many of the beliefs you store there, and use to make decisions, are false. Your Circle of Influence placed those beliefs there when your belief in your Circle of Influence was greater than your belief in yourself.

Everything and everyone you came in contact with, from birth until now, influenced you in one way or another. Family, friends, teachers, movies, television, radio, sight, sound, touch, taste, and smell became your Circle of Influence. Their influence shaped how you think and react to everything. So if your Circle of Influence taught you things that are true, and things that are false, about yourself and the world, then you can see how important it is to have a way to know the difference between what is true in your life and what is false.

You use those beliefs to judge yourself and everything and everyone around you. Your idea of the world is based on beliefs and judgments you made in your past.

Your Circle of Influence placed beliefs and judgments in your mind such as, "You're not good enough, you're awesome, don't touch that--it's hot!, a cold drink on a hot day is nice, don't swim after you eat a heavy meal, you're too dumb, you can do better than that, or you're brilliant." The list of beliefs and judgments has no end because your Circle of Influence keeps adding to it.

So you base all you know, do, and say, on your past emotional experiences. Such experiences are either true or false. Your survival depends on knowing which experiences are true, which are false, and what you want in life. You must learn to believe in yourself more than you believe in your Circle of Influence.

If you do not believe in yourself more than you believe in your Circle of influence, your Circle of Influence will confuse you by what it says to you and about you. You will forget it's okay to have and believe in your own ideas and thoughts.

Even when you have your own ideas and thoughts, you may not dare to say them, because your Circle of Influence, the people whom you like, love, and trust with your ideas and thoughts, may laugh at you or criticize you.

If you cannot trust your Circle of Influence with your ideas and thoughts, without fear of laughter or criticism, then you must change your Circle of Influence.

If you do not know which way to turn, and an emotional emptiness fills your heart and mind, then you fear your Circle of Influence will not accept you. That fear created your emotional emptiness.

When two or more questions, or two or more directions, relating to the same subject face you, and you do not know which question to believe, or which way to go, you have

## Self-Doubt

True Friends Praise And

Promote You, Even To

Those

Who Doubt You.

# 3

# Self-Doubt

## Recognizing And Destroying Self-Doubt.

## Recognizing Self-Doubt

Self-doubt happens when your Circle of Influence says you cannot do something, and you believe what your Circle of Influence says. So, you quit trying. You do not try to find out if you can do it or not. Why do you quit? Because your Circle of Influence taught you, and you trust what they say to and about you.

That trust created your self-doubt. Self-doubt makes you feel the

49

people in your Circle of Influence are better or smarter than you.

But the truth is this--their own self-doubt drives them to find and point out your limitations. So the question is, what makes their opinion of what you can do, right, and your opinion of what you can do, wrong?

## Destroying Self-Doubt

Once you understand that self-doubt comes from your Circle of Influence, and the fear of rejection comes from those you love and respect, you can take control of the emotions they now control which hold you prisoner.

All your decisions come from what you believe. The more connected you are to who you are, and what you truly want, the less you will care about what your Circle of Influence believes or says.

WHY?
BECAUSE IF THEY DON'T LIKE IT, THAT'S JUST TOO BAD!
WHY?
BECAUSE IF THEY DON'T LIKE IT, THAT'S JUST TOO BAD!

You need to say that powerful statement for the rest of your life, and you need to say it loud. You can probably say that statement right now about some things in your life. But your greatest challenge will be to say that statement about things in your life in which you are not sure. The good news is that only you have to know about this challenge.

51

So open your mind and challenge yourself. Stand and fight. Fight for your right to believe in yourself, your ideas, your life, your hopes, and your dreams--no matter what your Circle of Influence says, thinks, or does.

Your opinion of yourself does not have to match anyone else's opinion of yourself.

Once you understand what is true, and what is false in your life, and you commit to what is true, you will have no self-doubt. Your present lack of ability to make great decisions will not exist. Making decisions will be easy because you will know what you want.

Then you will face other fears like, "What am I going to do? I'm too old, too young, too tall, too short, too thin, too heavy, too uneducated . . . "

Your list of excuses has no end, because it comes from everything your Circle of Influence has ever taught you about yourself. And it all started the first day they saw you.

Remember--the longer your Circle of Influence controls your emotions, the longer you will avoid making decisions in your life. And the stronger and more intense your fear will be about making decisions. After a while, you will not be able to make decisions at all.

You will become powerless to move toward your goals and your dreams because you do not control your emotions. Your Circle of Influence controls your emotions.

A negative Circle of Influence creates self-doubt. This negative Circle says you can't reach your goals, your dreams, or your desires in life. You believe in your negative Circle of Influence more than you believe in yourself. Your negative Circle began creating your self-doubt on the day you were born.

You say you are not sure about that? Ask yourself these two questions:

Have you ever wanted to wear or buy something, and didn't, because you thought someone might make fun of you or criticize you?

Have you seen someone do something and thought, how could they do that in public? I could never do that. I would die of embarrassment!

If you answered "Yes" to either of those questions, you fear your Circle of Influence will judge you. That fear is a factor in every decision you make.

Until you break free of the control of your Circle of Influence, you will keep going round and round, spinning out of control in mind and spirit. You will fill with self-doubt. You will drift in a sea of emotional turmoil, not knowing what to believe, or which way to turn.

To destroy self-doubt, learn how your Circle of Influence triggers your emotions and controls you.

Learn your Trigger Points, learn how your Circle of Influence controls you through them, and you take the first step toward destroying your self-doubt.

Your Circle of Influence causes your self-doubt every day by pressing your emotional hot buttons. Every day, these emotional hot buttons, these

Trigger Points, control your emotions, your decisions, and your life.

# Trigger Points

No One Can Make You

Laugh

Or Cry, Angry Or Happy,

Run Or Stand Paralyzed

With Fear, Without Your

Permission.

# 4

# Trigger Points

## How They Steal Your Dreams, And Who Uses Them.

Your mind is like a novel. Every day, your experiences write a new page in that novel. Every day, your subconscious mind stores that page. As in all great novels, events happen in your life that you will never forget. These events change how you see the world, and how you see yourself fitting in, or not fitting in, to the world.

When you talk about "The Good Old Days, or The Glory Days," you activate bookmarks of the positive memories in the novel of your life. When you talk about those wonderful days, your words are long and warm, and your mind flows with memories that please you.

But when you talk about negative memories, your words are short, cold, and brittle. Your mind, body, and face are tense with emotion.

All memories, positive or negative, are Trigger Points. Like bookmarks, these Trigger Points activate the defining moments in your life. You base all of your decisions on your emotional reactions to those memories.

From birth to death, your subconscious mind processes and stores information about your emotional reaction to those memories. Whether your reaction is sad or happy, calm, or outraged, past memories trigger those reactions.

Why do you have Trigger Points? What do they do? What is their function in your life?

Trigger Points are links to emotions designed to protect you, and help you make decisions based on past life experiences. So you can see how important it is to understand which beliefs are true, and which beliefs are false.

Most people do not know they have Trigger Points. They do not understand how Trigger Points work. They do not know the devastation which positive or negative Trigger Points can cause in their lives.

You base everything you do on three emotions--**pain, fear, and pleasure**. These emotions control what you do every minute of every day. These emotions determine where you go, how you feel when you get there, and how you feel when you leave.

How you relate to pain, fear, and pleasure is very personal. So personal, in fact, that you hide your true emotions from other people so you won't be vulnerable.

That's why understanding who you are, and who is in your Circle of Influence, becomes so important. When you control your Trigger Points, you take away the power your Circle of Influence has over you.

So how you react to pain, fear, or pleasure each day determines your relationships, your financial future, and how you will live the rest of your life. Whoever controls your Trigger Points controls your life.

When you have false beliefs about yourself, who you are, and who is around you, you put your trust in people who have their goals in mind, not yours. People in your Circle of Influence may not know or understand what a Trigger Point is, but they know how to use them against you.

People who use your positive or negative Trigger Points against you are not your friends. They may say they love you, and are trying to help or protect you. They are not. They are controlling your emotions, hopes, dreams, and future to reach their goals.

They care nothing about your goals.

Ask yourself this--do people in your Circle of Influence control your

Trigger Points? Do they control the emotional outcomes of your life? Or do you control your Trigger Points to propel yourself toward your goals?

Only you can answer that question.

Do you feel your Circle of Influence uses your false beliefs and Trigger Points to hold you prisoner? Do you want to break free of their chains? Do you want to take control of your own life, and move toward your own goals?

Then let's get started!

First, you cannot erase a memory. You can, however, change your emotional response to that memory. So, if your emotional reactions control how you make all of your decisions, and all of your emotions, positive or negative, are word or action activated, then anyone can control your emotions simply by how they speak or act around you.

So when your Circle of Influence says or does something that triggers an emotional response, that emotion comes from a past experience. You will base your response upon pain, fear, or pleasure. You will either retreat from that conversation or action, or you will expand into that conversation or action.

No matter what that emotion is, it is your emotion. It does not matter if anyone else understands it, because they did not live your life. You did. So don't expect anyone else to understand.

However, your emotions determine how you will react, and what decision you will make, to the person who activated your Trigger

Point. You may not remember your past experiences connected to that Trigger Point. But your subconscious mind remembers because it never forgets and never sleeps.

So the better you become at knowing who you are as a person, what you want to do with your life, and what you want from your life, the more control you have over your Trigger Points, and your emotions linked to those Trigger Points. This control lets you make better decisions in and for your life.

But until you have a better understanding of who you are, what you want to do with your life, and what you want from your life, you will not know if your Trigger Points are working for you or against you.

That's why negative Trigger Points are so dangerous. Many

experiences you've had, many beliefs about yourself, are not true. Yet, you use these false beliefs to make decisions that determine the course of your life every minute of every day.

You must find those false beliefs and eliminate them from your life.

You can compare your mind and emotions to a computer.

Do you upgrade your computer with new files and programs and delete old files and programs that are no longer relevant? Does your computer then work better?

The answer is yes.

Would your mind and emotions work better if you upgraded them with new files and programs?

The answer is yes.

You have many things in your mind that are not relevant, never were relevant, and are not true any more. As your life changes, so does the information you need to guide you through your life.

To maximize your computer's use, you upgrade it. To maximize your life, you need to upgrade how you think, and how you feel, about the events in your life.

First, find a new program to do what you need done, in, and for, your life. Then simply install that program in your mind, just as you would install a new program in your computer. Your mind's new program will help you reach your goals, and make you more marketable. The more marketable you become, the more value you have for yourself and your world.

That new program will keep you up-to-date, moving in a forward direction, and let you think and work more efficiently.

Next, look in your mind and emotions for what is not useful to you. Delete those emotions from your memory. Get rid of them any way you can. That information is not relevant to you in your life any more.

In fact, your old, outdated files are where your Circle of Influence gets all of its power to use against you in the first place. Those old, outdated, emotional programs and files will keep you from achieving your goals while you build someone else's goals.

How do you recognize and change your emotional responses to your negative Trigger Points?

Simply become totally aware of your reaction to what is being said, or done, around or to you. The more intense, or out of control, your emotional reaction is to what is being said to you, or done around you, the easier your Circle of Influence can control your emotions and your life.

The greatest challenge you will ever face is not finding your negative Trigger Points--it is controlling your emotional reaction to them, because they are part of your current belief system. So, to change your reactions to your negative Trigger Points, you must face, challenge, and change your own beliefs and disbeliefs. This is very, very hard. But you can do it.

People just like you change their reactions to their negative Trigger Points every day. Listen to tapes and CDs. Read books. Go to seminars.

Surround yourself with a better Circle of Influence.

But know this--negative Trigger Points are very powerful, and your emotions can be very dangerous. Emotions can bring the greatest warriors to their knees, never to lift their heads up again from defeat. Emotions can bring the meekest people to fists of rage, to fight for a cause they believe in and will die for.

That is the power of triggered emotions.

If you are not aware of triggered emotions, and their power over you, someone else is aware of your triggered emotions, and will use those emotions to get you to do what they want.

When you let other people control your emotions, they control your time, thoughts, and life. You waste valuable time and energy. Not being in control of your emotions leaves you filled with pain and frustration, staring down a dead-end street, not knowing, or understanding, where to turn or what to do next.

Negative Trigger Points are your enemy, so it is important to deal with them. If you do not find and deal with your negative Trigger Points, people will control your ability to make decisions forever. Why do they want to control your Trigger Points and your emotions? They want to control you and your life so they can feel empowered. These people are

## Dream Stealers

Learn To Build A

Great Future In Spite Of

Those Who Doubt You.

# 5

# Dream Stealers

## They Make You Doubt Yourself Until You Stop Trying.

Dream Stealers hold you prisoner. They not only steal your hopes, your dreams, your desires, they steal your life by keeping you from achieving your goals. Dream Stealers find your fears, your negative Trigger Points, and use them against you.

That statement leads to a profound conclusion:

## WHAT YOU HIDE FROM,
## YOU BECOME A PRISONER TO.

That is where Dream Stealers get their power. They are masters at sensing and finding your fears, your Trigger Points. They need that power over you, because making you weak makes them strong and keeps them empowered. Being aware of Dream Stealers can save your sanity and change your life forever.

Dream Stealers began their criticism of you at birth. You came into the world ready to learn. But before you even knew what they were saying, you learned their body language and their tone of voice. They would gather around you and tell you how tall or short, thin or fat, beautiful or ugly, smart or stupid, strong or weak, or cute or plain you were.

As you grew and learned the language, your Circle of Influence taught you how to criticize not only other people, but how to criticize yourself.

Your Circle of Influence helped you form opinions and beliefs about yourself before you could even defend yourself. Adults brought you up to respect your elders. If you disagreed with them, or did not respect them, they punished you.

You felt powerless, rejected, punished, controlled, over and over again. You held in your embarrassment until you accepted it, or exploded in anger. Both reactions stopped you from achieving your dreams.

Beware of your negative emotions. Over time, your emotional distress becomes accepted and expected as normal. You become complacent about it, and do nothing to change it. Your dreams start to slip away.

The emotional beating you believe you must endure is another false belief the Dream Stealers ingrained in you because their Dream Stealers ingrained it in them. Negative in, negative out. How do you break the emotional chains which Dream Stealers use to imprison you?

How do you find and change your emotional response to your negative Trigger Points?

You learn about yourself and how you react to your Circle of Influence. Once you know and understand what you truly want in life, then, with great ease and self-assurance, you will make great decisions.

# Decisions

Awakening Your Body, Mind, And Spirit To The New World That Is Your Soul.

# 6

# Decisions

## Your Decisions Today Determine Your Successes Tomorrow.

Your past decisions have brought you to this point in your life. If you are happy with your life, close this book and keep doing what you were doing.

But if a nagging voice inside you says, "There must be a better way," you have admitted your need to make new decisions in, and with, your life. Life changing decisions. Decisions that will increase your zest for life, and your ability to enjoy that new life. Well, the good news is, there is a better way, and you can make better decisions.

When you first start making these decisions, it is extremely important to have patience with everything you do, or try to do.

But, most of all, it is important to have patience with yourself.

If you can do this simple task, if you can have patience in all things, your achievements will increase dramatically. Every time you choose to make a decision to live the possibilities of your life, your choices and your decisions will bring forth new and empowering beliefs and abilities in yourself that will help you make great decisions--decisions based on truths, not opinions.

Basing your decisions on truths is important. If you have the facts about yourself, and what you want, you will never again be at the mercy of anyone with an opinion about you, or what you should do.

Just remember--when you are face to face with two or more opinions about the same subject, you may take the two opinions too close to heart, or you may become too emotionally involved, leaving you with mixed emotions. You will then find it difficult to commit to any large or small decisions you make.

You should make all decisions with no emotions, because the daily choices you make determine what you will have and how you will live.

On life's highway, it is not what you drive that matters the most. It's what *drives you* that matters the most.

83

True genius is knowing and applying the difference between the words of the slow lane, and the words of the fast lane. This is your key to your personal freedom.

If you criticize, condemn, and complain about everyone around you, then negative people will expand into your life. Your words and your actions will give them comfort. This is the slow lane.

But if you praise and promote everyone around you, then positive people will expand into your life. This is the fast lane. This is the lane of the Dream Builders.

It all starts with being aware of your Circle of Influence. Truly listening to what is being said to you, and around you, will change your life forever.

It's about discovering your emotions, and making a decision to destroy the negative emotional trigger points that cause your self- doubt. Destroying your negative trigger points lets you rid your life of its Dream Stealers.

The first step to a fuller, richer life is making decisions.

Making clear decisions will enable you to create an "I can" attitude. Then you can build your self confidence, your future, and achieve your goals.

# Building Confidence

Be Willing To Go Over,

Under, Around, Or

Through

Anything that Stands In

Your Way.

# 7

# Building Confidence

## Developing An "I Can"
## Attitude

So, are you ready? Are you ready to take a stand? Ready to change your life? Ready to change your future? If you are ready, then let's change your life forever. The journey will not be easy, but it will enable you to achieve your dreams.

As you begin this journey, you may find yourself saying, "What if I make a mistake? Or fail? I could lose everything! It's too dangerous! What will people say? What will they think? No, I can't do it. It's just too risky."

Actually, the opposite is true about mistakes. It is more dangerous, and there's more risk involved, when you do not make mistakes.

It's not the end of the world if you make a mistake. Remember--as long as you keep trying, you can't fail.

Here's why--gathering and processing information is the first step toward true wisdom. But true wisdom comes from applying knowledge, from discovering what works for you, and adjusting what does not work for you.

That's why you need the proper Circle of Influence around you--to help you understand just how important mistakes really are in your life.

When you can adjust knowledge into wisdom, you will be able to climb or break through all emotional walls and barriers.

When you learn the power of a mistake, it will set you free. Free to be who you truly are. Free to achieve your heart's desire.

Unfortunately, today's world says mistakes are bad. And the world punishes you for making mistakes. When you feel the punishment connected with your mistakes, you become emotionally blind to the wisdom hidden within them.

That emotional blindness robs you of your confidence, your self-esteem, and leaves you with the crippling emotions your Circle of Influence uses to create your self-doubt--unless you grew up in a positive Circle of Influence, or you found a Circle of Influence which celebrates you. A positive Circle of Influence will help you learn that the power hidden within a mistake can force you to think in ways you never thought possible. A positive Circle of Influence will challenge you, dare you, to expand your ability to think beyond where you are now.

The key word here is "Help," help you understand. Then, and only then, will you discover the power, the magic, and the wisdom hidden in every mistake.

Just remember--every person who points at you, and laughs at you for making mistakes, makes mistakes, too. The difference is this--you are learning and gaining wisdom along the way to help you change your end results.

Those who point and laugh at you will make the same mistakes over and over again until they either learn to adjust their current system, or die. They keep on punishing themselves and criticizing everyone around them in a desperate attempt to make themselves feel better.

Because of the years of punishment everyone around you has placed upon you for so long, their words of criticism still control your life. Even though some of the people from your negative Circle of Influence are not even around you any more, their words echo in your mind.

Why? Because every time you make a mistake, you use the words they taught you to use on yourself, criticizing, condemning and complaining to yourself about yourself constantly. Now do you still wonder why you're not happy?

You're punishing yourself for your own mistakes.

You're so good at punishing yourself, that you fill your life with the self-doubt that your negative Circle of Influence taught you until you believe everything they said about you. All by yourself, you are shutting down your ability to think beyond your mistakes, without any new help from your negative Circle of Influence.

This fear, this self-doubt, holds you back from who you really are, who you really want to be, and what you really want to do with your life. This self-doubt leaves you frozen, paralyzed, and powerless.

The power, the magic, the wisdom you gain when you listen to your mistakes enables you to change your life and your beliefs in yourself. It is this knowledge and wisdom that creates your freedom to achieve that which you desire.

It will allow you to stop caring what others think about you. It will allow you to make great decisions with no regret, no retreat, and no surrender. It will set you free to achieve your goals. To enable you to live your dreams and visualize your future.

So if you see someone make a mistake, just smile, give them a pat on the back, and say, "Don't beat yourself up over this. It's a mistake, and we all make them."

Mistakes are costly. But they are the only true opportunities you have to gain the wisdom you need, so you can adjust what needs to be adjusted within yourself, so you can move on.

Never stand and stare at a mistake. Listen to it. Learn from it. Figure out what it's trying to tell you. Then adjust your strategy. Don't look back. Throw down the mistake. Get rid of it. Press on. Learn and adjust as you go.

Standing in one spot and staring at a mistake is insane. And you know what the definition of insanity is--

Doing the same thing you have always done, and expecting a different result.

You may say, this all sounds great, but how do I get started? Where do I get the information I need?

Five basic rules answer this question. (1) Shut off your television for one hour each day. (2) Use that hour to read books or listen to tapes or CDs. (3) Use that hour to go to seminars. (4) Use that hour to get near people who are alive with life. (5) Use that hour to go out into the world, to look around, and to have some fun.

There are people in this world who build amazing things in and with their lives. The difference between you and them is this--they find and associate with the Dream Builders of the world. So can you, if you decide to.

Dream builders love life and its challenges. They spend their lives looking for people like you so they can show you how you can build your dreams, too. They know that, together, anything is possible.

## Dream Builders

Their Words Of

Inspiration

Ignite Your

Imagination

And Inspire You

To Experience Your

Life

In Your Own Way.

# 8

# DREAM BUILDERS

## They Empower Your Passion To Live Life And Reach Your Goals.

Dream Builders praise and promote you, even when you do not want to hear it, even when you do not believe it, even when you doubt it--and yourself. Dream Builders understand self-doubt because they experienced it first hand. They know the power of a dream. They know what believing in each other can do. You see, believing in each other creates the awesome power that makes your dreams come true.

If there were no dreamers in this world, there would be no airplanes, automobiles, computers, cell 'phones, or all the rest of our modern inventions. Do you think these inventions, and others like them, came into existence without dreamers to build them?

Do you think everyone said, "You have a great idea!"

No way.

Ever since there have been dreamers, there have been Dream Stealers telling dreamers they were crazy. They were wasting their time. That's what Dream Stealers do. They hide behind their lack of ability to do things by putting down your ideas, and your ability to do what you want to do with your life.

Many things we use every day never existed until someone had a dream, stepped up to the plate, and said, through all their self-doubt, "I can do it." Those Dream Builders started listening only to their own inner voice, and stopped listening to the Dream Stealers.

The Dream Builders listen only to their own desires. They kept on going toward their goals through their self-doubt, and the Dream Stealers crying out, "You'll never do it! You'll never make it! You're wasting your time!" Through all of this, the Dream Builders changed your world, how you see your world, and the history of your world.

The bottom line is this--the bigger and greater the dream, the more violent the opposition you will face from friends, family, from anyone who couldn't find or believe in a dream if they tripped over it. Now the big question is this--how many of these people are guiding you through your life?

So build up some defense. Stand up inside yourself and shout from the rooftops, I will not be denied! This is my life, my dream. No one will ever hold me back again. I make this promise to myself--no regret, no retreat, no surrender.

It's time to start taking action in your life for your ideas, your dreams, your hopes, and your desires. It's time to start running toward your goals, and embracing them with passion, determination, and drive. So much passion, determination, and drive, that your Dream Stealers will run home with the same fear they have been putting in you all these years.

So run, run like you've never run before. Never give in, never give up, and never surrender. It's your will against theirs. Do not stop applying your ideas, your hopes, and your desires. If you stop building your dreams, the Dream Stealers win, and you will stop moving toward your dreams.

The best way to defeat the Dream Stealers is to stop listening and start acting. Become a Dream Builder and start taking action now.

# Love Life's Challenges

## Taking Action

I Am Gifted With 24 Hours Each Day. How I Spend Those Hours Determines How I Will Live My Life. I Will Not Be Denied That Which I Seek.

# 9

# TAKING ACTION

## Set Goals And Run Toward Them

## With Passion And Determination.

Taking action is about moving in a forward direction toward your goals. A key to taking action is to develop systems that work for you.

To understand what systems are, and how they work, you need to realize that everything you do, everything you have done, everything you ever will do, has a system hidden within it.

All systems have an order and a sequence. You use that order and sequence every day of your life.

From brushing your teeth to cleaning your house, building wealth, or building a skyscraper--every action and every thing has a system.

You reach your goals by creating and using systems that work for you. The better your systems work for you, the greater your results will be.

Remember--it takes patience, hard work, and studying what is happening within your life, and your systems, to discover how to adjust them to make them work best for you.

If you seek help from qualified people to develop systems that work for you, remember that the final decision to use, or not use, a system is yours alone. No matter what you are told, or how much pressure you feel, no matter how much controversy you face from your Circle of Influence, only you can decide to use, or not use, a system.

How do you find people to help you adjust the current systems in your life?

Ask yourself this basic question--do the people you consult have in their life what you want in your life? If your answer is yes, ask them how they got what they have, and how long it took them to get it. If their answers to these questions fit into your beliefs and your value system, then start applying their answers and their systems to your life.

Next, listen to their words. Listen to what they are saying to you and about you. If they are saying the same old things, if their answers leave you feeling flat, and make you want to quit, make you feel you cannot accomplish your goals, then run for your life. Find Dream Builders who will praise and promote you, your ideas, and your dreams. Find Dream Builders who leave you refreshed, energized, alive with life, and feeling like you can conquer the world. Because, if you believe you can conquer the world, you can.

These are the people who will ask you if they can help you develop new systems. They will help you stay focused on your goals. They will help you move in a forward direction.

They know you must have a written time frame for your systems to work for you to enable you to achieve your goals.

For instance, let's say you have decided on a system of saving money that works best for you. Let's say you give yourself six months to save a thousand dollars.

But you are unsure about getting started. You're thinking, what if I fail? What if I cannot reach my goal?

That's why it's so important to have a system, a team, so that you're not alone. You need people to bounce ideas around with. You need people to help you get rid of the situations that keep popping up. So, if you do miss your goals, you'll be strong enough to reset them. If you miss your goals again, you reset them again and again and again until you do reach your goals.

The process of setting and resetting your goals allows you to learn where and why your systems are working for you, and where they are working against you.

As long as you keep fine-tuning your systems, you cannot fail. That's right, you cannot fail.

Why? Because failure happens only when you quit doing what it takes to be a success. That's why being aware of your current systems is so important.

You will see where your systems are working for you, where your systems are failing you now, and where they might fail you in your future.

Then, and only then, will you get the results you need to achieve your goals. When you learn how to use and adjust your systems to move you toward your goals, your success will happen.

So how do you know? How can you tell if your current systems are working or not?

Ask yourself this--are you living the life you thought you would be living right now? Do you have the things you thought you would have at this point in your life? If not, then you are working a system that is not working for you. It is failing you.

So how do you change your current systems so you do not fall into the same old traps that keep you a prisoner?

Stop listening to the Dream Stealers of the world who tell you, "That's life. You won't ever get ahead."

Start listening to the Dream Builders of the world who tell you, "Adjust, adjust, adjust your current systems so you can achieve your goals."

Start listening to the Dream Builders of the world who say you choose the life you live by the choices you make. If you're not happy with your current life, change it. Change it by reading books, listening to tapes or CDs, and by going to seminars.

## Dream, Do, Live

Dream the dreams you need to dream, do the things you need to do, so you can live the life you want to live.

Turn off your television for one hour each day. Use that hour to feed your brain. Read a book. Listen to a tape or CDs. Go to a seminar. But, most of all, set new goals. Get out and have fun. Fill your mind with fresh ideas while you build your new life.

Only you can change your life. So go for it. Do not wait another minute. Take action now. The freedom and happiness which defines your life, and how you will live it, is on the line here.

Imagine your life is a business and you are the CEO. What decisions could you make to have your life, your business, run better? What could you do differently? Not tomorrow, not next week, but right now to make your business, your life, flourish in today's market? If you only learn one thing, make it this:

# YOU GET ONLY ONE CHANCE TO MAKE A GOOD FIRST IMPRESSION.

You Are Your Own Business

**The Most Valuable Person**

**You Will Ever Represent**

**Is Yourself.**

# 10

# You Already Own
# Your Own Business

## Your Clothes, Your Words, And Your Actions Are That Business.

You are your own business. How you dress, how you act, the words you use, how you treat other people, are all part of your business.

These things reflect who you are, and how serious you are about your business success. People notice such things. They especially notice how you respond to them as your customers.

Have you ever been in a store and could not find what you were looking for? Finally, you find and ask a clerk for help. But the clerk is busy, distracted, answers you abruptly, and gives you nothing for your efforts but annoyance and frustration.

How did you react? Did you leave that store simmering with anger? Did you promise yourself that you would never go back to that store again? Did you think, how could anyone treat a customer like they treated me? Who would hire such a clerk? How unprofessional can a person get?

Well, there are only two types of people and businesses in this world-- the kind you like to do business with, and the kind you do not like to do business with.

What would you say about the clerk, the customer, and the business you just read about in the previous paragraph? Would you like to be that clerk or that customer? Would you like to own that business?

If you were an employer in today's marketplace, would you hire you? Do you keep yourself—your business--competitive in the modern world? Do you keep yourself marketable? Do you read books, listen to tapes or CDs, or go to seminars? Do you do fun things to keep your mind fresh and your spirit alive?

In today's marketplace, it is vital to keep doing positive things for yourself, your business. Remember, the only one who can do positive things for your business is you.

For example, would you agree that you smell like whatever you bathe in? If so, do you think people go toward you, or away from you, according to how they feel about that smell?

Then, isn't it also true that bathing your mind in positive things draws people toward you, while bathing your mind in negative things pushes people away from you. Wouldn't the way you dress, your actions, your clothes, the words you choose, the way you treat people, also draw people toward you, or force them away from you?

Remember, negative in, negative out, positive in, positive out.

Only you can control your future. You choose what you read, what you listen to, and what seminars you go to. When you bathe your mind with positive thoughts, you draw people toward you, and you maximize your ability to achieve your goals.

The only difference between people who live their dreams, and people who wish they were living their dreams, is this--the people who are living their dreams came to a point in their lives when they said, "Enough! It's about time. It's about time I take the first step to achieving my freedom and my goals for my life." These people accept nothing less than achieving their goals.

So the real question is this--are you ready? Are you ready to say, "It's about time to start living my dreams. It's about time to be who I need to be, to do what I need to do, to have what I want to have in my existence."?

Well, it always comes down to your commitment to taking the first step.

Remember--the only thing you cannot change in your life is time spent.

But you will maximize your future, and your life will change, when you decide to change your life.

# Dream Big!  Run Fast! Challenge Life!  Go For It!

It's About Time

We Cannot Change Time Spent. But With Faith, Courage, And A Dream, Every New Horizon Is Like A Breath of Fresh Air, Filled With Wonder, Hope, New Vision, And Opportunities.

# 11

# It's About Time

## Seize The Moments Of Your Life.

You are gifted with twenty-four hours each and every day. So the single greatest and most incredible gift you could ever give, or be given, is the gift of time.

When someone shares time with you, that gift is priceless because they can never recapture that time spent. So the more time two people share, the greater and more incredible the gift becomes.

Time is the benchmark by which we measure all friendships and relationships. The greater and more intense the time spent, the greater the gift becomes.

So cherish those who spend time with you, for they are sharing the most incredible gift they possess.

It does not matter how significant you are, or how insignificant you feel you are in this world. It does not matter if you are homeless, or if you are a world leader. You are gifted with the very same twenty-four hours every day.

What you choose to do with those twenty-four hours will define the life you will live, and determine the level of happiness you will experience in your life.

That brings us to beliefs. Your amazing beliefs guide you through each and every moment and decision you have ever made, and each and every moment and decision you will ever make in your life.

This is important, because every time you make a decision or a movement, you are spending the only thing you can never recapture--Time.

That's why understanding who you are, and the effects your beliefs are having on your life, is so important. Remember, you are guided by two different types of beliefs--true beliefs and false beliefs.

# That Is Why The Single Greatest Thing You Will Ever Know

# Is Yourself.

We cannot change time spent.

But with faith, courage, and a dream, every new horizon becomes a breath of fresh air, filled with wonder, hope, and new visions of endless opportunities.

Always Remember The
Medicine Of Life--Live,
Love, And Laugh Like
There Is No Tomorrow,
Because You're Definitely
Worth It!

# Conclusion

## You're Awesome, And
## You Can Do It.

No one who was afraid to take a risk, or was realistic in their thinking, ever accomplished anything significant.

So the real question here is, Are you ready? Are you ready to stand up on your own and take on the world? Are you ready to take on the responsibility of being aware of who's around you, and what effect they're having on your life?

Are you ready to change your Circle of Influence where it needs to be changed, no matter what? Are you ready to recognize and destroy your self-doubt? Are you ready to stop and push away those Dream Stealers who tell you that you are not worthy of your own thoughts, your own ideas, and your own dreams?

The Dream Stealers know they are slamming your negative trigger points, time after time, just to get a reaction out of you. If they cannot control your emotions, their own need to control someone's emotions will force them to move on.

But understand this--if they have been controlling your emotions for a long time, they will not give up easily. There is a war out there, and you're the ground zero target. What's at risk is your heart, your mind, and your spirit!

So remember--no one has ever won a war without true passion for their cause. As you fight for your emotional freedom, the Dream Stealers will run right around behind you, telling you, and anyone else who will listen, that you have not changed one bit. They are just trying to hold you back. So the more they try to convince you that you have not changed, the more you know you are changing.

Oh, they'll tell you they're just trying to knock some sense into you, to save you. Save you? Save you from what? Yourself? Your dreams? Your hopes? Your desires? What you really want in life? That's not saving you. That's holding you back--and it's time you put a stop to it!

It's time to achieve what you really want in your life. Let your dreams, your hopes, your desires, become the biggest part of your life. Go for it! What's the worst that could happen to you? You might fail. Well, if you never stop trying, you can't fail.

So never, never, never stop trying. Never quit, and you will never fail.

Press on! Shoot for the sky! Start reading and learning new and exciting things from people who are alive with life and with life's endless possibilities.

I hope that, at least one time in your life, you get to sit in a room full of people who are alive with life, itself. People who can fill your mind, your heart, and your spirit with the endless possibilities and opportunities that await you. Once you believe in yourself, you can achieve anything.

This is the most incredible time in the history of the world to be alive and build your dreams. Why? Because you're alive, and you can achieve your dreams.

Set new goals in your life for your life. Read books. Attend seminars. Listen to tapes or CD's that really will change your life. It all starts with a decision. I hope your decision to start is today. I hope you decide, today, to seize the moments of the rest of your life.

# You're Awesome, And You Can Do It!

Knowing And Understanding That It's Okay To Be Who You Are, And That Your Opinions In Life Do Not Have To Match Anyone Else's, Will Give You A Newfound Freedom.

# Recommended Reading

(1) Fish

Stephen C. Lundin, Harry Paul, & John Christensen

(2) Gung Ho

Ken Blanchard & Sheldon Bowles

(3) High Five

Ken Blanchard & Sheldon Bowles

(4) It Only Takes A Minute To Change Your Life

Willie Joley

(5) Personality Plus

Florence Littader

# Recommended Reading

(6)  Reject Me, I Love It
John Fuhrman

(7)  The Five Love Languages
Gary Chapman

(8)  The One-Minute Manager Meets The Monkey
Ken Blanchard

(9)  Who Moved My Cheese?
Spencer Johnson

(10) Yes Or No
Spencer Johnson

# Recommended Viewing

(1)  A Beautiful Mind

   Russell Crowe


(2)  Bagger Vance

   Matt Damon


(3)  Dead Poets Society

   Robin Williams


(4)  Good Will Hunting

   Robin  Williams


(5)  Horse Whisperer

   Robert Redford

(6)  October Sky

   Jake Gyllenhaal

# Recommended Viewing

(7) Patch Adams

Robin Williams


(8) Pay It Forward

Kevin Spacey


(9) Seabiscuit

Jeff Bridges


(10) With Honors

Joe Pesci

**Prisoners of Our Own Beliefs** takes you on an extraordinary journey through time which lets you see how your past affects your present, and may negatively affect your future--unless you take action, now!

In reading this book, you will find a new way of thinking--and understanding--that lets you make decisions based on true beliefs in your life, not false beliefs.

That understanding is the key you need to focus your awesome potential, and to build the life you have always dreamed of--a life of love, passion, and the desire to embrace life's challenges with determination.

So, are you ready? Are you ready to unlock your awesome potential, today, right now?

Then let's get started!

**Gary Parent** is dyslexic and "aged out" of Orono High School when he was 20 years old. Until the age of 46, he never read a book. But he always kept reaching for his dreams. He has been a gravedigger, sign painter, martial arts instructor, and business owner. He is also an artist. With this book, he is now an author. *Prisoners of Our Own Beliefs* is Gary's first book--but not his last!

**To see more books like this, please visit our website at <u>www.network3000publishing.com</u>!**

Printed in the United States
202290BV00002B/106-210/A